D1315099

Embroidery Machine Essentials
Quilting Techniques

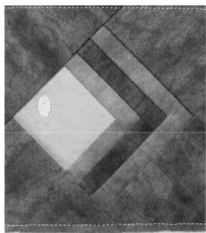

Linda Turner Griepentrog

©2004 by Linda Turner Griepentrog
Published by

An F+W Publications Company

700 East State Street • Iola, WI 54990-0001
715-445-2214 • 888-457-2873
www.krause.com

Our toll-free number to place an order or obtain a free catalog is (800) 258-0929.

Library of Congress Catalog Number 2004100742

ISBN 0-87349-846-1

Edited by Jeanine Twigg
Designed by Marilyn McGrane

Printed in the United States

Acknowledgments

This book has come together through the generous efforts of many industry companies that deserve thanks. Kudos go to Viking Sewing Machines for the loan of a machine for sample making. Sulky of America provided the threads used throughout the samples and projects. Oklahoma Embroidery Supply & Design donated stabilizers to keep the projects pucker free. Nancy's Notions provided the generous selection of notions necessary for great project results. Ackfield Wire donated the wire quilt hanger; Charlescraft, the towel blanks; Judi & Co., the black tote handles; Kaleidoscope Kutz, the photo image for fabric printing; and Sudberry House, the wooden box.

Thanks to the following companies for sharing their embroidery designs shown on samples throughout this book: Amazing Designs, Baby Lock, Brother, Cactus Punch, The Embroidery Resource, Oklahoma Embroidery Supply & Design, Tina's Cross Stitch, and Viking Sewing Machines.

Thanks also to Melinda Bylow for illustrations and Jeanine Twigg for embroidery design digitizing.

Dedication

This book would not be in your hands today had it not been for the encouragement and support of my husband Keith, who urged me to "Just do it!" He made numerous trips to my sewing room to see what I'd stitched out and to tout its marvels. Intrigued by the entire machine embroidery technology phenomena, we often discussed the answers to my favorite thinking-outside-the-box query, "What do you think would happen if I…?" The folks at the nearby fabric store also welcomed his hurried presence close to closing as he ran to get me something I might run out of in the wee hours stitching!

My two dogs, Winston and Riley, dutifully sat at my feet while the machine hummed—thinking attention should turn back to their needs and if dogs could talk, I'm sure they'd have asked "When will this be over, Mom, you just keep making *more* stuff?"

Speaking of moms, I'm sure my mother had no idea where my life would end up as she taught me to sew at a very early age. Thanks, Mom, for getting me started.

No credit list would be complete without dear friends who kept close watch on my book progress and sent unending warm fuzzies—life coach, Susan Voigt-Reising; *Creative Machine Embroidery* editor, Annette Bailey; *Sew News* contributing editor, Janet Klaer; *Windsor Oak* publisher, Donna Babylon; and *Total Embellishment News* publisher, Pauline Richards.

Much appreciation goes to Jeanine Twigg, who taught me the basics of machine embroidery, and never once laughed when I asked her some of the haunting "What if…?" questions. We continue to inspire each other to new embroidery challenges.

Cactus Punch design

Table of Contents

Foreword

The *Embroidery Machine Essentials: Companion Project Series* was created to provide you with easy-to-stitch embroidery designs and creative techniques to help develop your embroidery skills. Through the Companion Project Series you'll discover ways of looking beyond the "face value" of a design to recognize creative embroidery potential in every digitized design available.

I've asked industry expert Linda Turner Griepentrog to show you some incredibly easy ways to mix embroidery with quilting. She has created some simple-to-quilt embroidery designs that can be used with a variety of techniques. Be sure to check out the instructions on the CD-ROM—Linda has created some really great quilting projects! It is with great pleasure that I introduce to you *Quilting Techniques* with Linda Turner Griepentrog!

Jeanine

Introduction

Welcome to the wonderful world of embroidery machine quilting! Sewing technology has come a long way in my lifetime. I started sewing on a straight-stitch-only machine when I was four years old. It's hard to believe the continuing leaps in sewing machine sophistication. Who'd have ever thought we'd be combining sewing, embroidery and computer technology into one high-tech machine. Like others, I constantly speculate about what's next—maybe a machine that cooks dinner while we sew!

Having worked for a quilting and patchwork company, and being surrounded in my daily job as editor of *Sew News* magazine with our sister publications, *Creative Machine Embroidery*, *Quilter's Newsletter*, *Quiltmaker*, and *McCall's Quilting*, it was a natural for me to think about combining embroidery machine technology with quilting.

Traditional hand quilters may be a bit hesitant to embrace embroidery machine technology for the quilting process, but for those with embroidery machines, the time has come to use your machines for nontraditional applications. The projects in this book are easily attainable and showcase a variety of quilting techniques. I've stitched many of the samples on white fabric, but encourage you to use the endless array of fabric colors available to you.

The exclusive embroidery designs on the CD-ROM have been developed for you to try the many quilting techniques I show throughout the pages of this book. I also embroidered some samples with an assortment of commercially available designs to show that just about any design can be used for embroidery machine quilting.

This book is not intended to be a basic embroidery machine or quilting primer. It assumes a basic knowledge of both. The purpose of this book is to inspire you to use your embroidery machine for quilting. You'll be pleasantly surprised at the fun, creative opportunities!

Linda

OESD design

Embroidery machine quilting isn't just easy—it's fun! This book was created to help you get started. Along with detailed instructions and lots of creative ideas, you'll find a CD-ROM with 20 exclusive designs and over 80 bonus stitch files for your quilting experiments. Once you've mastered the basics, there are thousands of designs for quilting available to you through your local sewing and embroidery machine dealer, independent digitizing companies, and on the Internet. The step-by-step instructions for making this quilt are available on the CD-ROM.

Getting Started—
The Essentials

Design on CD-ROM

Embroidery machine technology has opened up a whole new world of creativity, especially for those who quilt. The machine can stitch designs quickly, automatically, and in multiples exactly the same.

There is a wealth of creative ideas for embroidery machine quilting. Choose quality digitized designs, embroidery supplies, and quilting supplies to help make your projects successful.

The 20 designs on the CD-ROM are available for your quilting pleasure. Each design has multiple stitch files and a perimeter baste to hold your fabric and batting layers together during the embroidery machine quilting process. For more information on using these and other quilting designs, see Chapter 2 starting on page 13.

Embroidery Supplies

The right embroidery supplies help ensure successful results. Like fabric, one can never have too much thread!

Hoops

Embroidery machine embellishing and quilting require the use of a hoop. The hoop supports the project fabric and stabilizer, allowing them to move together in a controlled manner as a design is embroidered.

Most embroidery machines offer a standard hoop size (4" square). Larger hoops are available and vary by brand. Check with your machine dealer for available hoop sizes and shapes. Depending on the size, multiple designs can be combined and embroidered in a single hooping offering a timesaving advantage.

Use the smallest hoop size possible for a single design. Too large of a hoop may cause fabric to slip or designs to distort during the embroidery process. If you plan to use your embroidery machine or specialty embroidery software to combine designs, use the hoop size closest to the actual design size or fill the entire hoop size with designs for embroidery.

An assortment of hoop sizes help the quilting process.

Threads

Machine embroidery threads are available in an assortment of fibers, weights, and colorations. The choice depends on the usage, desired visual effect, and care.

The most common thread is rayon, noted for its beautiful sheen. Polyester thread is colorfast and should be used on frequently washed quilt projects. Cotton thread offers a matte finish and is perfect for heirloom or vintage quilt projects.

Metallic thread can be used to add sparkle to designs. Choose openwork or outline designs as opposed to solidly filled designs for use with this delicate thread. Enlarging a design can help add "breathing room" for stitches to form ensuring successful embroidery results. Metallic thread quilting can be subtle or contrasting, depending on the color contrast to the face fabric.

Light-weight monofilament, or invisible thread, works well for allover quilting and is the best choice when prominent stitching lines are not desired. Available in clear and smoke and in both nylon and polyester, this thread is the perfect choice for embroidering across multiple fabric colors.

There are two specialty threads that add fun to quilting. Glow-in-the-dark thread appears white or pastel when embroidered, but once exposed to light, some brands will "glow" for up to 8 hours. Imagine the fun you can have stitching stars on a child's quilt!

Ultraviolet-activated thread is also a fun choice for quilting projects, especially for children. The thread appears as white or pastel indoors, but when exposed to sunlight it quickly changes to a brighter hue—either a pastel or a much more intense version of its original color. Envision a wedding dress with a white-on-white quilted train that blooms when the bride goes out to a garden reception.

Specialty bobbin thread should be used for embroidery machine quilting. Fiber contents include cotton, polyester, and nylon. It is available most often in black and white, although colored bobbin threads are becoming increasingly available. Convenient pre-wound bobbins are also popular, but check with your machine dealer for compatibility.

If both sides of the finished embroidery will show, choose a 40-, 50- or 60-weight embroidery thread the same or similar to the upper threads or that matches the backing fabric. If you plan to cover the embroidery underside with another layer, the bobbin thread color is irrelevant.

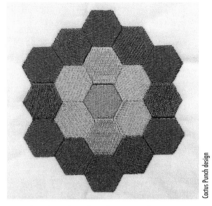
An assortment of threads range from small spools to large cones.

Motif embroidered with rayon thread.

Cactus Punch design

Variegated metallic thread creates an elegant block.

Design on CD-ROM

Linda says

For best results using metallic threads for quilting, use a needle especially designed for metallic threads. This needle type has a larger eye, scarf, and front groove to help prevent abrasion during the embroidery process. Slow the machine speed during embroidery. If the thread is on a small spool, consider using a thread holder placed behind or to the side of the machine to allow for a longer delivery path and time to "unkink" before reaching the needle. Some tension adjustments may be needed for successful stitching.

Design on CD-ROM

Metallic thread quilting.

OESD design

Underside of the design with and without color-coordinating.

Colors

Any quilting design can blend or contrast with the base fabric color, depending on the desired visibility of the stitches. Threads can be lighter or darker than the base block fabric, similar in tone, or invisible; each creates a different overall look for quilting.

Variegated thread offers the most versatility when embroidering single-color outline designs. Assortments of colors change throughout the thread strand as the embroidery design stitches. The number of colors and the length of each color vary amongst manufacturers. Some brands have a seamless variety of colors where others have a defined break at each change in color.

Most embroidery threads are available in both solid and variegated colors on spools and various size cones, depending on the brand. For thread colors that are used often it is more economical to purchase thread on cones with more yardage.

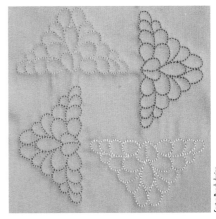

Choose threads for quilting depending on the desired effect.

Weights

Machine embroidery threads are available in a variety of weights ranging from size 12 to size 100—the higher the number, the thinner the thread. Most embroidery designs are digitized for 40-weight rayon thread. Any variation from this weight may require design or machine tension changes.

Heavier thread weights are most often used with outline quilting designs to make the stitches more prominent, or to fill in space when a design is enlarged beyond its original digitized size. Two lighter weight threads can be used through the same needle eye to increase the stitch weight for outline quilting designs. Use a larger size needle for this technique.

Stitch the same design in various thread weights—top to bottom: 12 weight, 30 weight, and 40 weight.

Linda says

To work with 12-weight thread:
- Test-stitch for design compatibility
- Use a size 100/16 sharp needle or a size 90/14 topstitching needle.
- Adjust tension if necessary.
- Choose simple outline designs; increase size to elongate stitches if necessary.
- For use with densely filled designs, enlarge the design at least 20 percent.
- Try using 12-weight thread for only a portion of an embroidered design, like the outline.

Needles

Matching the type and size of needle to the thread and fabric ensures embroidery success. It's important to select a needle that will allow the embroidery thread weight to easily pass through the eye and fabric without damage to either.

Most needle brands show a dual sizing notation with the metric size listed first followed by the American sizing. Needles are available in sizes 60/8 to 110/18—the larger the number, the bigger the needle shaft. For most embroidery machine quilting, select a sharp, universal point or machine embroidery needle. The point on a universal needle is slightly rounded, but it is usually sharp enough to penetrate a woven fabric without damage. A machine embroidery needle has a special scarf (the shaping on the back of the needle just behind the eye) and a larger eye to prevent thread shredding and breaking—look for these in various sizes.

Topstitching needles offer a larger eye to prevent fraying when using heavier threads like 12- and 30-weights. When quilting through dense fabrics, thick batting, or embroidering over multiple seam layers, use a special quilting needle designed with a long tapered point.

Linda says

Change needles frequently during the quilting process, as synthetic batting and stabilizers can dull needle tips.

Stabilizers

An assortment of stabilizers from a variety of manufacturers is available.

A stabilizer is used behind fabric to help add firmness and stability during the embroidery process. Embroidering designs on single-layer woven fabric blocks requires the use of a tear-away stabilizer to support the embroidery stitches. Embroidering a layered block or quilt does not require additional stabilizer as the batting and backing support the stitches.

To stabilize a single-layer woven block fabric, choose a tear-away variety in a weight that will support the embroidery stitches. Hoop the stabilizer and the fabric together, embroider, and then tear away the excess stabilizer around the motif.

If the quilt fabric has a surface texture, such as fleece, velvet, corduroy or terrycloth, choose a water-soluble stabilizer film for use as a topper. The stabilizer goes between the embroidery design and the fabric surface to keep stitches from sinking into the texture. After the embroidery is complete, tear away the excess stabilizer, or remove according to the manufacturer's instructions.

Scissors

Curved tip, sharp point embroidery scissors are essential for trimming close to embroidery threads and jump stitches. The slightly curved tip allows the blades to reach the design while it is still hooped and on the embroidery machine. Pull jump threads up with a tweezers and snip thread close to the fabric.

A sharp, quality pair of embroidery scissors will make snipping jump stitches or loose threads a breeze.

Linda says

After cutting jump stitches (those small thread connectors between embroidery sections), use an adhesive lint remover to pick them up and keep them from being caught in future stitching. When the adhesive outer layer is full of thread clippings, just peel to expose a new layer.

Fabric Markers

A water-soluble or air-disappearing marker allows for temporary design placement marks on fabric. Air-disappearing marks disappear within hours or days, depending on the humidity; water-soluble marks disappear when rinsed or spritzed with water. *Note:* If the marks are pressed with an iron before removal, they may be permanent. Test markers on scrap fabric before starting a project to check for compatibility. Ink colors vary amongst manufacturers. Most common are white ink for use on dark color fabrics, and light color ink for use on light color fabrics.

Temporary Spray Adhesives

This "can't-do-without" notion is used to temporarily adhere stabilizer to fabric for embroidery. It's perfect for sandwiching nonfusible batting to the quilt face and backing. Some temporary spray adhesives disappear over time or wash-away during laundry.

To use, place the item to be sprayed in a deep-sided box to protect surrounding areas from overspray and lightly spray the item. Spray only the stabilizer or batting; do not spray the face or backing fabric.

Another option for protecting surrounding areas from overspray is to make a cardboard shield the shape of the inner hoop by 6"-10" tall depending on the hoop size. Tape the cardboard ends together and place the shield in the hoop while spraying adhesive to avoid adhesive build-up on the exposed hoop surface.

Quilting Supplies

With so many wonderful tools and supplies available for quilting, visit your local quilt fabric shop for the latest in must-have supplies.

Fabrics

Almost any fabric can be used to create an embroidered quilt—the most common are the beautiful cottons and flannels in prints or solids. More unusual fare can be featured as well, like satins, velvets, and wool. Traditional cotton quilt fabrics come in a limitless number of colors, as do embroidery thread colors. No two quilts will ever be the same!

For best results, choose high-quality fabrics that will withstand some hooping force. The thinner the layers the easier it will be to quilt. If there are hoop marks after embroidery, steam creases away with an iron. To avoid compression, do not press the quilt layers .

To shrink or not to shrink fabric is a question with varying answers. Many prefer to prewash fabrics and batting to avoid subsequent shrinkage and prevent color bleeding. Others like the vintage look and choose to wash the quilt after it is finished. For more on Vintage Quilting refer to page 25.

For solidly embroidered blocks, it is best to prewash fabrics and batting to avoid design distortion. Simple outlines embroidered through all the layers can be embroidered on washed or unwashed fabric depending on the technique.

Embroider on the unusual—even silk!

Battings

Batting comes in a variety of fibers, finishes, colors, and weights. They're available by the yard, precut from craft size to king size in white, black, gray, or ecru. Personal preference will be your guide depending on the desired look and hand of the finished quilt or garment. For embroidery machine quilting, it's best to use a batting no more than ¼" thick.

Polyester batting is light-weight compared to its cotton or wool counterparts in similar weights. It washes and dries well and is easy to machine embroider quilt. Look for polyester batting that is bonded—coated with a thin layer of resin to prevent fiber migration during wear. When using a nonfusible batting, use temporary spray adhesive to secure layers together, or pin/baste in place.

Cotton batting is very suitable for machine embroidery quilting. It tends to weigh more than its polyester counterpart and dries slower after washing. It also shrinks up to 10 percent, making presoak-

ing necessary if a vintage look is not desired for the finished quilt. Cotton batting comes in two colors—white (bleached) and ecru (natural color).

Needlepunch, fleece (not the outerwear ilk), sweatshirting, or flannel work well for embroidery machine quilting. All are thin, yet provide a durable inner layer without added bulk. These are especially good for quilted garments, where excess bulk may not be flattering. Presoaking will eliminate shrinkage.

Fusible batting is a great choice for embroidery machine quilting and embellishing. The light coating of adhesive on both sides holds the backing and face fabrics in place with only a shot of steam. This simplifies the layering and hooping process by eliminating basting threads or pins. The slight stiffness created by the fusing agent can be rinsed for a softer hand.

To use, position the quilt or block right side down on a flat surface, cover with batting, and add the quilt/block backing

A variety of batting fibers and weights is available.

fabric right side up over the batting. Fuse the layers in place with bursts of steam from an iron.

Fusible fleece is lighter weight than batting and is fusible only on one surface. It is suitable for fusing the face fabric to the filling. The quilt backing is added after the embroidery is complete. Because of the weight, it's perfect for quilted garments without adding bulk.

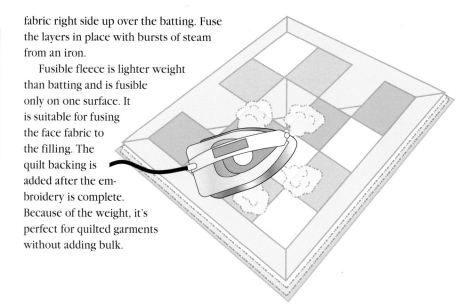

Commonly Used Terms

Here are some quilting terms to help guide you through this book. For a comprehensive list of embroidery terms, refer to the CD-ROM in Jeanine Twigg's book *More Embroidery Machine Essentials.*

Backing: The fabric on the quilted project underside, usually a contrast to the face fabric. Backing can be added either before or after the embroidery process.

Batting: The middle filler layer of a quilted project, sandwiched between the face and backing fabrics. The filler can be various types and weights including flannel, needlepunch or other lofty fabric.

Block: A small fabric section, usually square or rectangular, that is combined with many other fabric blocks to form the upper layer (face) of a quilting project. Blocks may be embroidered before or after quilt assembling.

Face: The uppermost fabric in a quilting project either comprised of pieces (blocks, crazy patch, etc.) or a single fabric piece (whole cloth). Also, referred to as the quilt top.

Piecing: The joining of small fabric sections in various shapes and sizes to create a larger section used as a quilt face fabric.

Quilting: The technique of joining the face fabric, batting, and backing fabric layers together with stitching. Quilting keeps the layers intact without shifting and adds decoration to the quilt.

Trapunto: The technique of adding dimension to fabric areas in an embroidered outline quilting design.

Whole-cloth: Face fabric comprised of a single piece of material (or one seamed for added width), but not decoratively pieced. Embroidered motifs create the quilting details.

Need Help?

In any embroidery adventure, your sewing machine dealer is the best resource to help resolve problems and answer questions about your machine, stitch settings, and less-than-perfect results—utilize this valuable resource. Machine company Web sites often have frequently asked questions (FAQ) and the answers to resolve brand-specific concerns. Also, machine embroidery magazines offer articles on specific techniques, design ideas, and problem solving.

Many sewing or embroidery machine dealers offer an embroidery club that meets on a regular basis to discuss embroidery or make projects. There may be a small fee for participation, but it's a great way to network with embroiderers who own the same machine brands.

Seeking advice from friends with embroidery machines, whether in person or online, can be your best lifeline. If only to find out you're not the only one who's ever made a mistake!

For more information on the embroidery process, refer to other titles in Jeanine Twigg's *Embroidery Machine Essentials* series.

Cactus Punch design

Chapter 2

A traditional choice for quilting are basic outline designs, but just about any design can be used for embroidery machine quilting. Whether decorating face fabrics or through all the layers, consider using embroidery machine quilting for all your projects especially with contemporary quilt trends. The step-by-step instructions for making this wallhanging are available on the CD-ROM.

Design Decisions

Just about any embroidery design can be used for quilting, whether to embellish a block, or in the process of quilting the face, batting, and backing layers together. Designs range from traditional outlines to solid fills. To further enhance a block, there are appliqué and motif-stitch designs available in contemporary to traditional themes.

Cactus Punch design

Stitch Options

There are many different types of designs available for quilting. The most popular, whether by embroidery machine or free-motion, is a continuous running stitch. For embroidery machine quilting, this type of design is referred to as an outline.

Outline quilting designs can be digitized with a single running stitch, double-stitch, triple-stitch (bean), and some with up to five stitches over the same line, making them appear bold against the face fabric.

Several more stitch variations are available for outline quilting designs—chain-stitch, motif-stitch, and blanket-stitch. A chain-stitch resembles a chain "link."

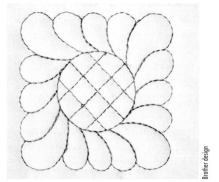

Brother design

Single-stitches embroidered with variegated thread.

Cactus Punch design

Triple (bean) stitches.

Cactus Punch design

Chain-stitches.

A motif-stitch resembles a decorative sewing machine stitch and can be available in any style. A small blanket-stitch resembles the hand sewn edging for blankets.

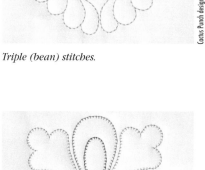

Cactus Punch design

Narrow blanket-stitches.

Embroidery stitches are determined by the design digitizing company. On the enclosed CD-ROM, you will find designs in multiple stitch variations.

Designs on CD-ROM

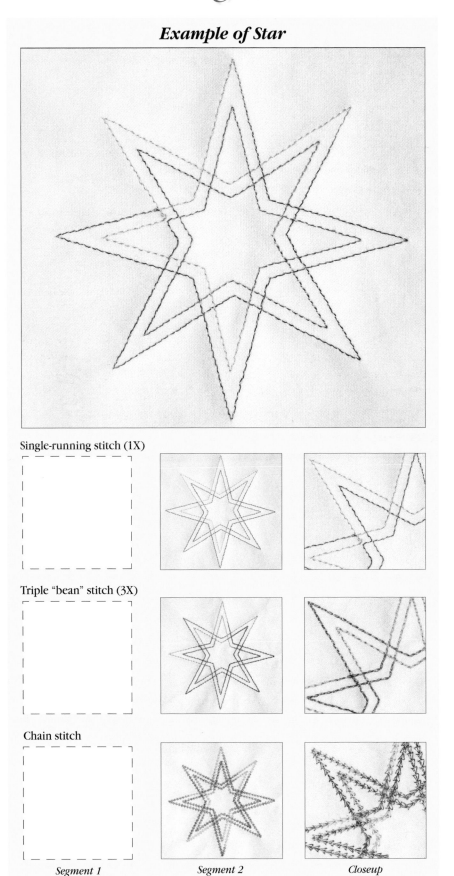

Example of Star

Single-running stitch (1X)

Triple "bean" stitch (3X)

Chain stitch

Segment 1   *Segment 2*   *Closeup*

For your convenience, the CD-ROM in the back of the book contains 20 exclusive embroidery designs. As an added bonus, each embroidery design has been created with additional stitch types and sizes. For example: one design may have up to three additional files each containing one of several additional stitches, like single, double, triple (bean), chain, or satin stitches. For more information about each design and the available stitches, refer to the Design Details starting on page 46.

All the designs offer a perimeter baste that stitches an outline around the design area prior to embroidery. The long perimeter basting stitches hold the fabric and batting or stabilizer layers together to help prevent shifting during the embroidery process. The first segment of each design is the perimeter baste and can be identified by the first thread color. To save a thread color change, use the same thread color as the design (segment 2).

To remove the perimeter basting stitches after the embroidery process, snip the stitches on the embroidery underside before unhooping the fabric. Snip every three to four stitches, and then on the fabric top, pull up on the top basting thread to remove the stitches. The clipped bobbin threads will poke up and can be removed easily.

If your embroidery machine has a perimeter baste built into the machine, skip segment 1 of the design and use the machine perimeter baste if desired.

Design Options

There are a variety of digitized designs that can be used for quilting.

Designs containing satin stitches can be used for embroidery machine quilting. Choose designs with narrow satin stitch widths that will allow larger areas of block fabric to show. This will provide block texture and batting to "puff" between the stitches.

Some fill-stitch designs can be used for embroidery machine quilting. The test-stitch process is important to determine if a fill stitch is appropriate to stitch through batting and fabric layers. Fill-stitch designs are generally used to embellish blocks prior to quilting.

Appliqué designs are popular for adding interest and color to quilts. These designs can be used to quilt through all the layers or embroider onto face fabric blocks. All appliqué designs have an outline stitch that is used to hold appliqué fabric to the block fabric. This outline can be used individually as a design for the embroidery machine quilting process. Simply stitch the outline design and do not stitch the remainder of the design.

Many designs have unique characteristics. From stippling to cross stitch, the sky is the limit to the availability of designs for quilting.

A satin-stitch design.

A fill-stitch design.

An appliqué design.

Stippling

Some outline designs even come complete with background stippling to fill the block. These designs are often used for the quilting process—stitching through the quilt face, batting, and backing layers. The entire design can be stitched in a single color similar to the base fabric color for a subtle look, in a contrasting color for more prominence, or a combination for added interest.

Stippling stitches fill the block surrounding the outline design.

Cross Stitch

For lovers of cross stitch by hand, the embroidery machine simplifies the process. Choose a cross stitch design and an even-weave fabric for stitching. When hooping even-weave fabric, it's imperative to line up the weave pattern with the hoop markings to avoid the motif appearing askew. Use scraps of even-weave fabric with different thread counts to test-stitch designs. This will help you determine which thread count matches best with the embroidered crosses. Some design manufacturers offer a recommended stitch count fabric. Using 30-weight threads for cross stitch helps to fill holes. In addition, the colors appear more solid than when using lighter weight thread.

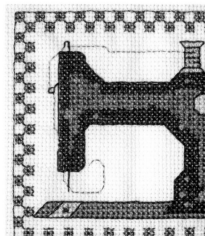

Cross stitch designs for the embroidery machine save time from tedious hand stitching.

Redwork and More

Simple outline designs depicting scenes from everyday life were originally hand-embroidered using a simple stem stitch to create Redwork, Bluework and Blackwork masterpieces. An embroidery machine can stitch single-color designs in a fraction of the time it would take by hand. Depending on the design size, choose a 40-weight thread, 30-weight for more prominence, or a 12-weight thread for the boldest impact. Choose thread colors based on your personal preference or the design theme.

Linda says

To extract an outline from a more complex design, advance through color changes until you reach the outline. This can also be accomplished using embroidery software. Delete all the segments from the design except the outline. Be sure to save the original design before making changes. Resave the design with a new name. For more information on using embroidery software, see Jeanine Twigg's *More Embroidery Machine Essentials* book.

Utilize traditional Redwork designs in the kitchen. Project instructions on CD-ROM.

Allovers

Allover patterning can be created from one design that is digitized to repeat when hooped continuously, or by combining several single designs. Individual designs can be repeated using the touch screen of your embroidery machine or in embroidery software. Using tone-on-tone thread colors for quilting can create subtle allover texture for connector blocks, individual blocks, and as a background for fill-stitch designs. Embroider continuously onto fabric or layers, and then cut blocks, sashing, or sections to be used for a project. Allover embroidery is great for garment quilting in cuffs, collars, or small pattern sections.

Allover design.

Purchasing More Designs

In addition to the designs on the CD-ROM, embroidery designs are available from sewing machine manufacturers, local retailers where embroidery machines are sold, independent digitizing companies, or on the Internet. Check with your local sewing or embroidery machine dealer for more information on the available selection of designs for your equipment.

Many companies offer embroidery designs in multi-format disk packs for those with computers. Know what file format your embroidery machine utilizes. Not all designs are available in every format. With the appropriate software, some embroidery designs can be converted from one format to another for your equipment.

Designs can be purchased individually or in disk packs on the Internet from machine company Web sites or those of independent digitizers. Look for sites that offer "search" options by topic or keyword. Enter the word "quilting" and discover thousands of available designs.

Embroidery digitizing software is available for the creation of designs from scratch. Some offer simplified auto-digitizing functions, while others require manual stitch creation. Outline quilting designs are among the easiest to digitize. See your local sewing or embroidery machine dealer for more information on digitizing software.

Designs can be purchased in many different sources. See Resources on page 45.

Cactus Punch design

Chapter 3

Stylized tabletop accessories are a great way to experiment with quilting techniques. Use one, two, or even four different techniques. The creative use of quilt components makes for a great conversation piece when friends or family come for a visit. The step-by-step instructions for making this gift bag are available on the CD-ROM.

Quilting Techniques

Cactus Punch design

The embroidery machine can be used for quilting in several ways. Embroider a design onto fabric (or a block), and then combine it with batting and backing to create a quilt. Or, embroider a design and quilt layers together in one process by layering the face fabric, batting and backing, and then embroidering through all three layers at once.

Test-Stitching

It's important to test-stitch designs before starting any embroidery machine project. The test-stitch process ensures compatible fabric, stabilizer, thread, and tension combinations to achieve successful results. The multiple layers of a quilting project make this process even more important.

Always test-stitch on sample fabric the same as the project until you are satisfied with the results. When evaluating a test-stitch sample, check for tension problems, design distortion, general stitching quality, and your thread color selection. If something is awry, embroider again until it's right, and then move on to the actual project. Test samples won't go to waste. They can always be used for future projects like ornaments, gift tags, or any number of pieced quilting projects. Keep nonuseable samples in a reference notebook with machine settings, thread type, stabilizer, batting, etc. for what not to do!

Cactus Punch design

Test-stitch designs on sample fabric before beginning any embroidery machine project.

Quilting Blocks

The process of joining multiple quilt layers can be easily and decoratively accomplished on the embroidery machine. Mark the design center point and cross marks on the face fabric with an air-disappearing or water-soluble marking pen. Layer the face fabric, batting, and backing layers together. Pin or fuse layers together depending on the batting used. For more information on quilting layers, refer to Chapter 4 "Putting It All Together" starting on page 32.

To hoop, place the outer hoop on a flat surface, and place the fabric and batting layers right side up over the outer hoop.

Place the inner hoop over the fabric markings aligning the cross marks with the hoop notches, and press the inner hoop firmly into the outer hoop.

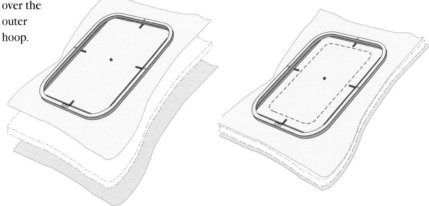

Do not stretch fabrics while hooping to prevent distortion. It may be necessary to loosen the hoop tension substantially depending on the thickness.

Select the desired design on the embroidery machine and prepare the machine for embroidery. The designs on the enclosed CD-ROM feature a perimeter baste to keep multiple layers from slipping. These securing stitches outline the area for embroidery. The stitches are later removed when the embroidery is complete. Some embroidery machines have this feature built in. If your embroidery machine has a perimeter basting stitch, skip the first segment of the designs.

Align the needle with the center point on your fabric and begin the embroidery process. When the motif is complete, remove the hoop from the machine and remove the fabric from the hoop. Rehoop and stitch the desired number of motifs needed for the quilt.

Use a single-stitch outline quilting design to fill a block.

Cactus Punch design

Appliqué Quilting

Embroidery machine appliqué is popular because it adds color and texture to block fabrics, reduces the stitch count, and emulates the time-consuming hand piecing of years gone by for quilters. Appliqué designs are quicker to stitch than those with fill stitches and more consistent for multiple designs than free-motion machine embroidery. Appliqué designs are available with an assortment of finishing stitches, such as satin, blanket, or motif edges.

There are a variety of embroidery appliqué methods; the most popular is the stitch-and-trim method with pre-programmed stops for appliqué fabric placement and trimming.

Appliqué the block with a satin-stitch edge finish.

Metallic appliqué fabric highlights a pair of sewing shears.

If the appliqué fabric is unstable, such as a stretchy knit, loose weave, or slippery metallic, back it with light-weight fusible interfacing to stabilize it for the appliqué process. Other options include using spray starch or a liquid stabilizer to add firmness.

Hoop either the block with a stabilizer or the layered quilt block, aligning the design center cross marks with the hoop notches. Cut the appliqué fabric larger than the design size and position it on top of the base fabric. Use temporary spray adhesive to hold it in position for stitching or double-sided adhesive fusible web. (1)

Stitch the appliqué guidelines—a single or double row of outline stitches. The machine will stop automatically when these stitches are complete. (2)

Remove the hoop from the machine, but *do not* unhoop the fabric. Using sharp, curved embroidery scissors, closely trim the excess fabric away from the stitching line. If you do not trim closely, the finished appliqué will have raggedy threads sticking out from the edge stitching. If you trim too closely, the outline stitches will not hold the appliqué fabric in place.

Return the hoop to the machine. Zigzag stitches will secure the appliqué fabric to the base fabric (3), and then satin, buttonhole, or motif stitches will finish the raw edges. (4)

If the design has more than one area of appliqué, repeat this process for each section. For more information on the appliqué process, refer to Jeanine Twigg's *Embroidery Machine Essentials Companion Project Series: Basic Techniques*.

A variety of fabrics for appliqué can be used. Be creative and choose unique fabrics from metallic to fleece for fun.

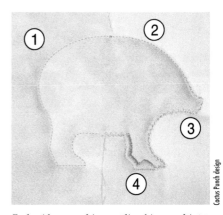

Embroidery machine appliqué is a multi-step process.

Pieced Appliqué

A more intricate and complex look can be achieved by piecing the appliqué fabric prior to stitching it to the base fabric. Simply join several narrow fabric strips right sides together, and then press the seam allowances in one direction. Be sure the pieced fabric is larger than the appliqué design size.

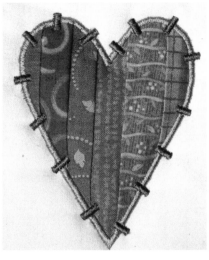

Viking design

Piece assorted fabrics together and use the "new" fabric for the appliqué.

Creative Appliqué

There are a variety of additional appliqué techniques that are fun to stitch by simply adding layers of fabric before quilting.

Place a layer of felt or felted wool on top of the block fabric and embroider an outline quilting design. Trim close to the stitches inside and out of the outlines for a dramatic block accent.

Place several layers of unwashed flannel onto the block fabric before quilting. Trim within the channels of a spiral design to create chenille. When the block is washed, the edges fray creating a fuzzy, fun look.

Add fabrics that fray to the block fabric before quilting. After embroidery, trim ¼" away from the stitching and allow the laundry process to fray the outer edges. This contemporary detail adds a raw edge to quilt tops.

Design from CD-ROM

Felted appliqué.

Design from CD-ROM

Chenille appliqué.

Design from CD-ROM

Fringed flannel appliqué.

Fabric Tinting Accents

The addition of color to outline designs can be accomplished above or below the fabric with colored fabric or batting.

Below the Block

Using a contrasting color fabric or batting behind white face fabric adds subtle interest to a block. Hoop the contrast fabric or batting under the face fabric during the embroidery process.

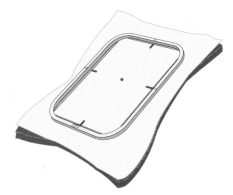

When the embroidery is complete, carefully trim away only the fabric or batting underlayer close to the design. To emphasize the color subtlety, back the face fabric with pure white batting before completing.

Deep fabric color shows through the quilting.

Above the Block

Add a bit of sparkle to a design by adding a sheer fabric overlay of organza during the embroidery process. Secure the sheer fabric in place with temporary spray adhesive. The sheer layer can be used under a section or the entire design. To use in only a design portion, stop the machine after stitching the designated section, trim the sheer fabric close to the stitching, and finish stitching the remainder of the design.

For more fabric detail accents, refer to "Mixed Media: Coloring Inside the Lines" on page 43.

Organza overlays the motif center.

Black batting shows through to highlight the outline quilting design. Project instructions on CD-ROM.

Background Quilting

Add interest to an embroidered block with background block stitching. The additional quilting prominence depends on the thread and fabric color contrast. To avoid a busy appearance, keep the thread and fabric color similar.

Shadow Quilting

To emphasize an embroidered motif, use a sewing machine to stitch a shadow outline very close to the outer edge. The width of a presser foot can serve as guide for stitching.

Motifs can be outlined with decorative machine stitches. Some designs even have one built-in.

Don't stop with just one row of stitching. Continue adding rows outward from the original design shape to the block edge.

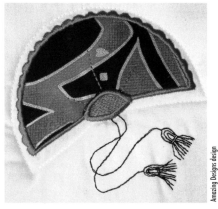

Use the presser foot width as a guide for shadow stitching.

A decorative stitch outlines the appliqué motif.

Parallel stitching rows echo the embroidered motif shape.

Decorative Stitching

Take advantage of the multitude of decorative stitches available on your sewing machine. Use one or more stitches to quilt the fabric background before embroidering a design. Choose embroidery designs that are densely filled to cover the stitching lines.

A decoratively stitched background highlights the embroidered motif.

Double Needle Quilting

Double needles can be used with outline quilting designs. They consist of two needles on a single shank with varying space between them. They are designated with two numbers, such as 1.6/70—the first number indicates the millimeter space between the needles and the second number denotes the metric needle size. Check with your machine dealer for compatibility before purchasing double needles for embroidery.

Each outline design embroidered with a double needle takes on a different look depending on the needle spacing and the stitch direction. Designs can be stitched with the same thread color through both needles or with contrasting colors. Depending on the contrast, the resulting motif may actually appear to be blurry or shadowed. The test-stitch process can help determine the desired appearance.

To use a double needle, use a second thread spool on another spool pin, or if your machine doesn't have two holders, wind a bobbin for the second needle's thread and place it below the spool on a single spool pin. Thread each spool through the machine to individual needles. Make sure the threads do not tangle as they unwind from the spools.

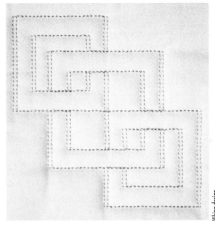

Double needle embroidery can result in a shadow effect.

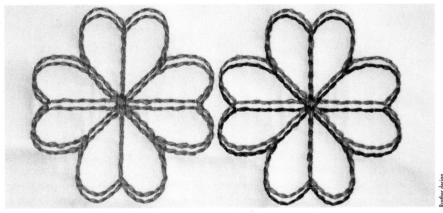

Use the same or different colors through double needles.

Vintage Quilting

Create a vintage look for your embroidered quilting project by taking advantage of fabric and batting shrinkage. When using this technique on a quilt or garment, allowance must be made in the project cut size to allow for the shrinking process. Some fabrics and battings may shrink up to 10 percent.

1. To test, layer a 12" square of 100 percent cotton fabric, cotton batting, and 100 percent cotton flannel backing.

2. Using embroidery software or on-screen editing, combine several designs to fill a mid-size (approximately 5"x7") hoop.

3. Embroider the design, unhoop it, and serge the edges of the layered square.

4. Using hot water, wash the embroidered sample in a regular wash cycle with towels or other garments of similar color range.

5. Run the sample and other items through a hot dryer cycle.

6. Measure the size of the shrunken sample to determine what allowance must be made for shrinkage when constructing the actual project.

Before washing.

After washing.

Stuffed Quilting

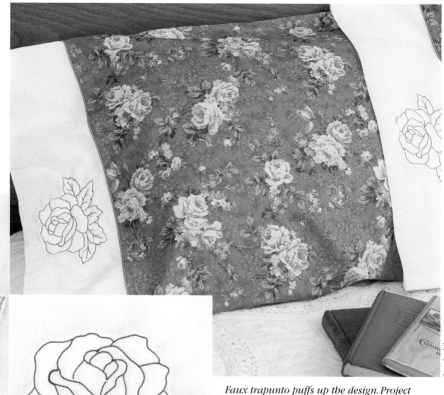

Simple outline designs are perfect for adding additional dimension, a technique called trapunto. Extra batting, fiberfill, or cord is used in design sections to make raised areas. Often combined with background stitches or stitches that surround design areas, the "stuffed" sections appear more prominent.

Faux trapunto puffs up the design. Project instructions on CD-ROM.

Trapunto

For traditional trapunto, embroider the desired outline design through only the face fabric and light-weight, nonfusible batting. From the reverse side, cut a small slit in the batting layer *only* under each area to be stuffed.

Using a tapestry (blunt point) needle or small crochet hook, poke bits of stuffing into the opening. Do not overstuff or the design will appear rigid. When completed, whipstitch the openings closed. Add backing fabric to complete the project.

Stuff portions of a motif for added dimension.

Whipstitch slits closed after stuffing.

Corded Trapunto

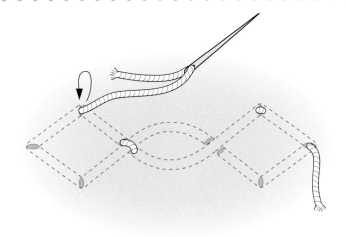

To stuff a design with cording, choose outline designs with narrow channels. Embroider the desired outline design through the project face and light-weight batting. To add dimension to narrow areas, thread yarn or soft cord between stitching lines and batting layers using a tapestry needle.

At the corners, bring the needle up through the backing and back down rather than trying to turn the corner within the channel. Clip yarn ends close to the batting. Add backing fabric to complete the project.

Front.

Back.

Faux Trapunto

Embroider the desired outline design through the project face fabric and one layer of medium-weight, nonfusible batting. When the embroidery is complete, trim the batting closely around the design area, leaving it within the design for extra loft. Add batting and backing to complete the project.

Extra batting raises the design center.

Pieced Blocks

Use an embroidered design as the focal point for a crazy quilt patchwork block. Strip fabric pieces together around an embroidered fabric to form the perfect frame for single designs. For a more intriguing combination, piece together velvets, silks, laces and ribbons, and add decorative machine stitching

Linda says

Pieced blocks are the perfect place to use test-stitching samples. Choose one, or use multiples that coordinate.

Randomly piece outward from an embroidered block center.

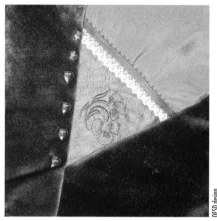

Add beads, lace and ribbon for a Victorian crazy pieced block.

Coordinating Fabric & Designs

Matching embroidery designs and fabric with a similar theme is a fun exercise in creativity! The list of possibilities is endless.

Use coordinating fabrics in borders and/or sashings to tie in a quilt theme. A picture says a thousand words!

Match fabrics to designs for theme blocks.

Foundation Piecing

Small fabric piece blocks are easily created using an embroidery machine and specially digitized designs. This technique is similar to foundation piecing using a sewing machine where strips of cotton quilt fabric are pieced together with embroidery machine stitches. Relax and have fun with this automated way to foundation piece.

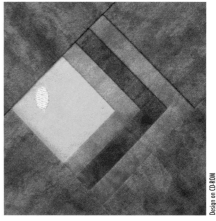

Foundation piecing using an embroidery machine.

1. Hoop the block fabric with batting. Instead of a perimeter basting stitch, stitch the entire design except stop just before the eye stitches. Use the same thread color as the block fabric. This step will help you identify the segments and location of the stitches, as well as hold the layers together.

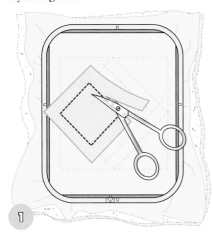

2. Cut a 3" square piece of fabric for the Fish face. Place the fabric over the small square area and stitch segment 1.

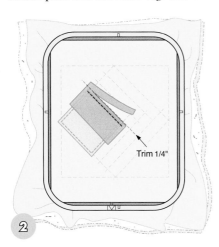

3. Cut two 1½" by 5" strips of each color fabric for the Fish scales. Place the right side down over the segment 2 line and stitch segment 2. Trim excess fabric away close (approximately ⅛") to the stitching line.

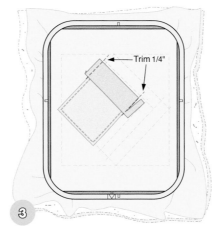

4. Remove the hoop from the machine; do not unhoop the fabric.

5. Finger press or use a craft iron to press the fabric to the right side. Trim excess fabric close to each end of the stitches.

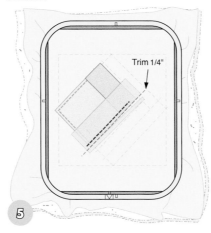

6. Return the hoop to the machine and stitch segment 3. Trim excess fabric away close to the stitching line.

7. Remove the hoop from the machine; do not unhoop the fabric.

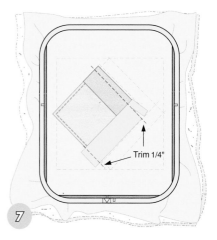

8. Finger press or use a craft iron to press the fabric to the right side. Trim excess fabric close to each end of the stitches and through the segment 2 fabric piece.

9. Repeat for segments 4 through 8. For the corner triangles, cut two 4" fabric squares. Cut in half diagonally. Use the triangles for each corner when stitching segments 9, 10, 11, and 12.

Crazy Piecing

Crazy quilting using an embroidery machine.

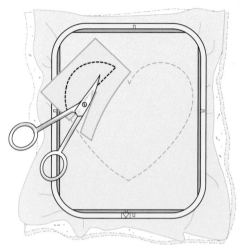

The time-honored tradition of crazy quilting with leftover fabrics can be easily achieved using an embroidery machine. Specially digitized designs with decorative stitches aid in piecing scrap fabrics to create unique blocks. This embroidery machine technique is similar to appliqué as the fabric scraps are trimmed to size before the decorative stitches are added. For best results while piecing, use clear nylon or synthetic machine thread to help hide the stitches among the variety of fabrics. Then, switch to thread colors that coordinate with the fabrics to secure the fabric with embroidered decorative stitching.

1. Cut 5 pieces of scrap fabric 2½" square.

2. Hoop the block fabric with batting. Stitch segment 1 (perimeter baste; optional) and segment 2 (heart outline).

3. Place piece of scrap fabric down onto the left heart side. Stitch segment 3.

4. Remove the hoop from the machine; do not remove the fabric from the hoop.

5. Trim close to the stitching outer edge.

6. Return the hoop to the machine and repeat this process until the heart is complete.

Design on CD-ROM

Combining Designs

A quilt block can showcase a single design or multiple designs combined within the block size. Measure the block size and allow at least ½" on all sides of the design for joining to other blocks. Always cut the block size larger to allow for the hooping process.

Using computer embroidery software offers more options like combining designs, adding lettering for personalization, reshaping, resizing, and altering design colors. Some embroidery machines allow for these limited design modifications on the touch screen without the need for a computer. However, embroidery software allows you to make design modifications with ease.

Combine designs on the touch screen of your embroidery machine or in embroidery software.

Combine individual designs to fill a block using the touch screen of your embroidery machine or embroidery software. Also, use the resizing, mirror imaging, and rotation functions to add interest to the grouping.

Corner designs can be combined to create totally new designs. Combine four designs to make a bordered block, or six designs to fill the open space. Add lettering or another embroidery design to the framed block center.

Enlarge, reduce, and rotate a single design to fit inside the hoop.

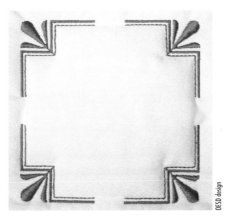

Combine four designs to make a block border.

Combine six designs to fill a block.

Lettering

Most embroidery machines have built-in lettering capabilities ranging from a few simple lettering styles to a multitude of alphabets. These fonts can be combined with your quilting designs, or combined with each other to actually become a quilting motif. Many embroidery companies offer a large collection of alphabets or monograms in both upper and lower case.

Think about using lettering in unique ways, and experiment with the mirror imaging, resizing, and rotating capabilities offered on your embroidery machine or within embroidery software.

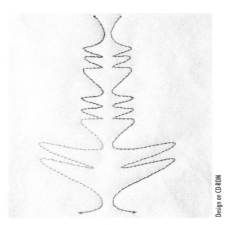

Use outline lettering for quilting.

Lettering can be added to embroidery for a label.

Chapter 4

After the embroidery machine quilting of blocks, it's time to put all the layers together. Use traditional piecing methods or experiment with creative construction ideas. The step-by-step instructions for making this wallhanging are available on the CD-ROM.

Putting It All Together

Cactus Punch design

There are multiple ways to use an embroidery machine to quilt through layers. The secret is in handling the bulk.

Cactus Punch design

Handling the Bulk

Managing the bulk of a large quilt project is a challenge for any type of machine quilting. The keys to success are simple. Use fusible batting to ensure all layers are kept together without slipping. If you're using a nonfusible batting, use temporary spray adhesive, safety pins, or hand basting stitches to hold the layers together. Pin outside the embroidery machine quilting areas or move pins as you come to them in the quilting process.

Support the weight of the project to avoid distortion during the embroidery process. Place the project bulk to the machine left and completely on a surface of similar height as the machine bed. Do not allow the project to rest on your lap or hang over the table surface. This will pull on the machine hoop and arm causing misalignment and distortion.

Corral the quilt portion not being embroidered. For a large quilt, roll up the excess bulk and use quilt clips to keep the roll secure. As you move to a different area of the quilt, re-roll, and re-clip as needed. When you're working in the center of the quilt, you may have rolled areas on both sides of the hoop, depending on the project size.

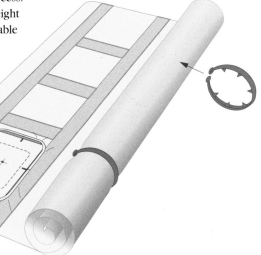

Keeping the bulk in check eliminates the hazard of catching part of the quilt under the embroidery hoop. On a very large project, enlist the help of someone to manage the bulk while you concentrate on the embroidery quilting stitching. Remember, the embroidery machine arm and hoop need to function unencumbered for proper stitch alignment.

Whole-Cloth Quilts

Layer solid face fabric, batting, and backing, and then quilt. Project instructions on CD-ROM.

As the name suggests, this technique begins with a single piece of fabric for the quilt face. The quilt can be embroidered through the face fabric and batting, or through the face, batting, and backing. If the embroidery is completed through less than three layers, an additional quilting process must take place to hold all the layers together.

When embellishing a whole-cloth quilt, careful marking must be completed before the embroidery process to ensure accurate placement of the individual designs. Designs can be placed all over or in a regular pattern to look like blocks. The latter placement often combines straight or decorative machine stitching to define block divisions and/or border sections.

Piece, Then Quilt

A variation of the whole-cloth concept is to piece unembroidered fabric blocks together to create the quilt top. Layer the quilt face with oversized fusible batting and backing; do not add the binding. Use fusible batting to hold layers together and sporadically pin the layers together for added security on larger projects. Hoop and embroider multiple outline designs of your choice in a pattern or randomly over the entire quilt. The embroidery underside is visible on the quilt back, so use matching thread for a unified finish. After the embroidery is complete, trim the batting and backing layers to match the quilt face. Bind the raw edges with bias fabric strips.

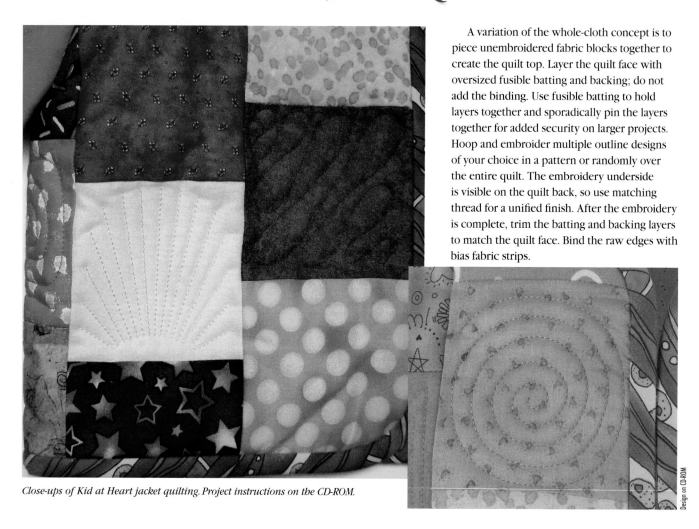

Close-ups of Kid at Heart jacket quilting. Project instructions on the CD-ROM.

Block-By-Block

Blocks can be embroidered through all the layers (face, batting, and backing) or through only the face and batting, with the backing fabric added later to cover the stitching underside. Embroidery designs can also be stitched on only the face fabric layer, with a tear-away stabilizer behind. When the embroidery is complete, the stabilizer is removed, and the blocks are sewn together and then layered with batting and backing. Depending on the embroidery method, you'll need to assemble and quilt the layers.

Single-Layer Blocks

If individual blocks were embroidered without batting or backing, cut plastic see-through templates in the desired block size, including seam allowances. Use templates to cut the required number of blocks from the embroidered pieces, centering the motif within each block. Cut sashing and individual border strips used to join the blocks together.

To assemble single-layer blocks:

1. Stitch sashing strips right sides together between two block edges, creating horizontal strips. Press seam allowances toward the sashings.

2. With right sides together, join longer sashing strips to the remaining block strip edges, aligning the previously joined blocks; press seam allowances toward the sashings.

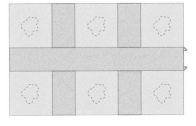

3. Add border strips to the outside edges of the block grouping.

4. To layer the quilt, place the quilt backing wrong side up on a large flat surface. Smooth the batting on top, and top with the quilt face right side up. For nonfusible batting, pin the layers in place. For fusible batting, follow the manufacturer's instructions to fuse the layers together, and then pin sporadically for extra security.

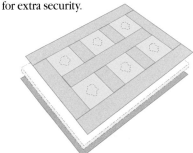

5. Quilt the layers together by stitching in the ditch of the seams. When complete, bind the quilt edges.

Multi-Layer Blocks

If individual blocks were embroidered with batting and backing, cut plastic see-through templates in the desired block size, including seam allowances. Use templates to cut the required number of blocks from the embroidered pieces, centering the motif within each block. To assemble layered blocks:

1. Cut sashing and border strips, doubling the number of strips required for the face.

2. Cut sashing and border strips from batting, one for each *set* of fabric strips cut.

3. Place one sashing strip right sides together with the embroidered square and top it with a batting strip. Position a second sashing strip right side against the backing fabric right side. This creates a sandwich of batting, sashing, block, and sashing, all raw edges together. Stitch the seam.

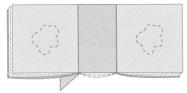

4. Add a second block in the same manner, but without catching the lower sashing edge.

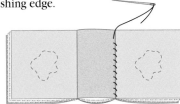

5. Turn under the cut edge of the lower sashing strip and cover the second stitched seamline; hand tack in place.

6. Continue adding blocks in this manner for both the vertical and horizontal sashings, aligning previously stitched blocks, until you reach the desired size.

7. Add border strips around the edges; baste unattached border edges together. Bind the quilt edges.

If individual blocks were embroidered with batting, but not a backing, cut plastic see-through templates in the desired block size, including seam allowances. Use templates to cut the required number of blocks from the embroidered pieces, centering the motif within each block. Cut sashing and individual border strips from the desired face fabric and batting used in the blocks. Sew sashing and borders onto the blocks.

When piecing is complete, cut a backing piece a little larger than the quilt top. Smooth and pin to hold layers together. Quilt the layers together by stitching in the ditch between seams. When complete, bind the quilt edges.

Border Quilting

There are many designs available for embroidery machine quilt borders. Designs can be stitched singly, in combined multiples, or resized to fit the desired border space. Borders are a great place to use the rotate and mirror-image editing functions on the embroidery machine or with software. To create a continuous border, combine designs end to end. Changes to designs can be made on the touch screen of the embroidery machine or in embroidery software.

Printing an actual size border design onto transparency film from embroidery software can make the placement process easier. Mark each design center point on the line using the template for perfect alignment.

Border corners can present design challenges. Options are to leave unembroidered corner space purposefully blank, overlap designs, filled with a different design than the border motif or repeat a design from a block on the quilt.

To start the border embroidery process, first determine the design size and the border length. Select a border design that can be embroidered multiple times to fill the space. For example, if a border area measures 30" long and the chosen border design is 3" long, it will require 10 adjoining designs to fill the space. Determine your largest hoop length and how many designs can be embroidered in each hooping.

To help with design alignment, draw a centering line the entire border length. This will be the placement line for the designs. Hoop a mesh water-soluble stabilizer, spray it with temporary adhesive, and secure the quilt edges to the stabilizer aligning the hoop notches with the placement line.

Stitch the first design along the line and use a template to mark the design centering point for the next hooping. Match the hoop notches with the long line and the needle position to the center for perfect alignment.

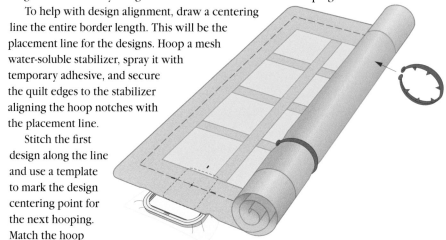

Another option for hooping border edges is to cut the border, batting, and backing pieces larger to accommodate hooping all the layers. After the border has been embroidered, trim to desired size, then bind.

Rotate designs to fit along border edges.

Cactus Punch design

Mirror-image designs to fit along border edges.

OESD design

Mirror-image designs and add connector designs to fit corners.

Cactus Punch designs

Linda says

Don't forget to support the weight of the quilt project on a large flat surface to avoid distortion during the embroidery process. Use bobbin thread to match the border fabric or the upper thread so the quilt reverse side will look finished.

Join designs for a continuous border—use the mirror-image function or abut in the same direction.

Design on CD-ROM

Quilt Labels

Many companies offer designs for making quilt labels. The labels can be embroidered directly on the quilt backing or on other fabric that can be sewn onto the backing as a patch.

Use the touch screen of your embroidery machine or embroidery software to personalize the label with your name, the recipient's name, date, or other sentiments. If preferred, use permanent fabric marker to add these details.

Instead of a label, hide your name on a block somewhere on the quilt top. As you're embroidering blocks, consider using the touch screen of your embroidery machine to program your name into a block pattern.

OESD design

Label your work as a family heirloom.

Design on CD-ROM

Add lettering to the frame using your embroidery software.

Embroidery Resource Design

Allover outline embroidery makes for fun piecing with coordinating fabrics. The step-by-step instructions for making this table mat or wallhanging are available on the CD-ROM.

Viking design

Chapter 5

Use your embroidery machine quilting for projects other than quilts. The multiple layering of fabric and batting can be easily applied to handbags, clothing, home décor and more. The step-by-step instructions for making this handbag are available on the CD-ROM.

Beyond Quilts

Viking design

The world of machine embroidery quilting can extend beyond the traditional venue of bed or wall quilts. Add embroidery machine quilting techniques to sewn garments, gifts, framed art, ready-to-wear blanks, home décor, and a host of other creative projects.

Garment Quilting

Most of this book has been devoted to quilt making. The same layering principles also apply to garments. The pleasure of garment quilting is that the overall pieces are smaller and not as cumbersome as a full-size quilt!

Piece blocks, and then quilt through all the layers. The step-by-step instructions for making this jacket are available on the CD-ROM.

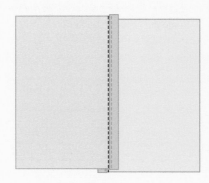

Keep these tips in mind for garment quilting:

- If possible, eliminate the side seam to avoid quilting over seams. If the side seam is straight, overlap the seam allowances to create a single-piece garment section. (Refer to Kid-At-Heart Jacket quilting instructions on the CD-ROM.)
- Preshrink all fabrics and natural fiber batting before cutting, unless you want the vintage look. For the vintage look on sewn garments, cut fabric sections at least 3" larger than the pattern on all edges to allow for the fabric shrinkage. Experiment by mocking up a 12" sample of fabrics and batting layers. Wash the sample to determine the rate of shrinkage. Build this information into the fabric and batting requirements for the project. (Refer to page 25 for more information on Vintage Quilting.)
- Interfacing isn't necessary in most garments that have been layered with batting and backing. If buttonholes are to be the garment closure, you may want to add a little section of interfacing for stability under buttonholes to prevent stretching.
- Choose needlepunch, light-weight fleece or flannel for garment structure without added bulk. For best results, use fusible batting or temporary spray adhesive to hold the layers.
- Serge or bind seams to flatten bulky seam allowances. Binding raw edges will also allow for reversible seams and garments. Overlap seam allowances and sewing on the original stitching line for a reversible fashion accent.
- If you prefer not to quilt an entire garment, consider quilting only a section like sleeves, collars, or cuffs. Use these sections in combination with melton wool or fleece for outerwear coats and jackets.

It's easy as 1-2-3 to quilt a garment

. . . .

1. Mark the design center placement on the garment. Cut a small piece of nonfusible batting or fleece slightly larger than the design area. Spray the batting with temporary adhesive and position behind the embroidery area.

2. Hoop water-soluble mesh stabilizer, spray with temporary adhesive and adhere the garment in place, aligning the design center point with the hoop markings.

3. Embroider the design, trim the excess batting around the design, and remove the stabilizer.

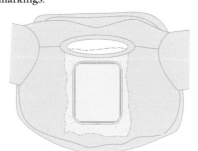

Embroidery on a sweater or shirt is easy.

Design on CD-ROM

4. To prevent irritation from the batting against the skin, fuse a piece of light-weight tricot interfacing over the embroidered area wrong side. Press lightly to avoid flattening the design. If the garment fabric is light-weight, pink the tricot edges to avoid show-through.

Not Quilted?

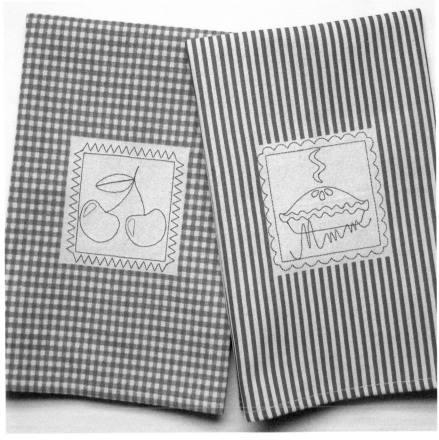

Outline quilting designs can be used for many other fun embellishing projects besides those with padded interiors. Think outside the box for multiple uses on non-traditional media. Always ask yourself the question, "I wonder what would happen if…?" and let your imagination run wild with the answers.

Any design you might use for quilting can also be used for non-quilting creations—just leave out the batting and backing! They're perfect for garments, home decor and giftables.

Embroider premade items for quick gifts. Designs on CD-ROM.

Mixed Media

Many outline designs used for quilting are simple in shape, with minimal stitching so they can be stitched on media other than fabric. Look beyond using thread to color in a design. Mix craft media instead like watercolor paint, fabric markers or even crayons to add a hint of color.

Metalwork

● ●

Embroidery on metal allows you to make unique creations that look like old-fashioned tin punching for ornaments or gift wrap tie-ons. To embroider on metal, choose a lightweight craft foil from your hobby store (our sample is a 36-gauge tooling foil)—in a weight that is soft and pliable. Foils come in brass, copper and silver, and some brands even come in colors. Use a large needle—size 100 or larger, and a piece of felt or fleece slightly larger under your hoop.

Outline quilting designs embroidered on metal make great holiday ornaments or package tie-ons.

1. Hoop adhesive tear-away stabilizer, or make your own by using a non-adhesive tear-away stabilizer and temporary spray adhesive.

2. Do not hoop the metal. Instead rough-cut the metal smaller than the hoop using old scissors; adhere it to the stabilizer.

3. This technique uses no thread, so it's necessary to override the automatic top and bobbin sensors by putting thread through all the thread guides; tape the upper thread above the needle; do not thread the needle.

Design on CD-ROM

4. Select an outline embroidery design with minimal stitching as too many stitches will perforate the metal and cause it to become distorted or ruined.

5. Place fleece or felt under the embroidery hoop to protect the machine throat plate from damage, as the underside of metal embroidery is sharp.

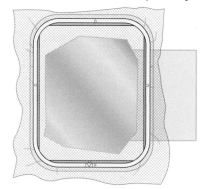

6. If your machine makes an automatic center stitch before the first embroidery stitch, advance beyond it to avoid a puncture in the design center.

7. Slow the machine speed, and embroider the design, stopping *before* the machine ties off at the design end and returns to the center point—skip those functions to avoid errant holes.

8. Carefully peel the metal off the stabilizer. Cut around the motif—use decorative scissors if desired. For an ornament or hanging tag, punch a hole through the foiling with an awl or paper punch and thread with ribbon or cord.

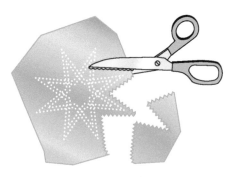

Linda says

Make a metal package tie-on from the same quilting design used on the gift inside the box!

Fabric Printing

Combine an outline quilting design with computer-printed images on fabric for the ultimate creation with technology. Specially treated fabrics are available for printing using an inkjet printer or a copier—check your local fabric, craft or office supply store for fabric availability. Virtually any fabric, even a print or texture can be prepared for printing with specialty liquid set and rinse agents.

For best results, follow the manufacturer's directions for printing, and then use any number of techniques to embellish the fabric. The fabric-printing image is on the CD-ROM for making the pictured Kaleidoscope Box. Refer to the project PDF file on the CD-ROM for more information.

Combine printed fabric with outline quilting designs for a high-tech creation; printable image, project instructions and design from CD-ROM.

Coloring Inside the Lines

The addition of paints, watercolors and crayons onto fabric with embroidered outline quilting designs, can be a fun way to go beyond the usual and into mixed media dimension.

Watercolor paints aren't just for paper. Watercolor your outline quilting designs by dipping your paintbrush into water, onto watercolor pods, and onto fabric. When your creation is complete, iron with a dry iron to set the paint into the fabric to render it permanent.

Crayons aren't just for kids. Lightly color your outline quilting designs with crayons, press with a dry iron with a paper towel on top for 5 seconds, and your crayon coloring is complete and permanent. Seek the help of kids for the ultimate fun in quilting mixed media creations.

Fabric paint and appliqué designs are the perfect combination. Skip the fabric. Instead, paint the appliqué area outline with fabric paint. Another option is to stitch all the appliqué outlines, paint between the lines, allow to dry, and stitch the edge finishing stitches.

Watercolor painting outline quilting design.

Color outline quilting designs with crayons.

Outline sections of appliqué designs are perfect for painting.

Paper Creations

Embroidering on paper can make beautiful stationery and cards, and quilting designs are a perfect choice as many have minimal stitch counts. Too many perforations can damage paper. Choose papers with a high fiber or rag content—you want substance, but not too many extraneous seeds or leaves will deflect the needle. Use a small size needle—size 70/10 is best to avoid leaving large holes in your work. Size 40 or 50 weight thread in any fiber, solid or variegated, is perfect for most papers. A size 30 thread and a slightly larger needle works on card stock or heavier papers.

If both sides of the paper will show in the finished project, experiment with a variety of light-weight tear away stabilizers including clear water-soluble stabilizer to hold the work in the hoop. Spray the stabilizer lightly with temporary adhesive and adhere the paper to the stabilizer. Make sure the stabilizer can easily be removed after embroidery. Select designs with minimal stitching and/or use only straight stitch outlines, depending on the weight of the paper.

As with metalwork, advance the stitches beyond the centering needle stitch and stop stitching before tie-offs to avoid errant holes. Embroider the design, and carefully tear away the stabilizer. Don't use water to remove it. Bring thread ends to the underside and lightly glue in place. Accent the embroidery by cutting the paper using decorative scissors or punches found at local scrapbooking or craft supply stores.

Outline quilting designs are perfect for stitching on stable papers.

Projects on CD

Step-by-step instructions for these 12 projects can be found on the CD-ROM.

Project 1   Door Hanger

Project 2   Tablemat

Project 3   Whole Cloth Quilt

Project 4   Kid-At-Heart Jacket

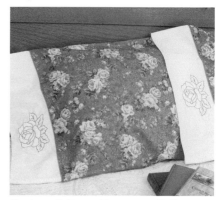

Project 5   Faux Trapunto Pillowcase

Project 6   Fringe Wallhanging

Project 7   Gift Bag

Project 8   Elegant Tote

Project 9   Kitchen Wallhanging

Projects 10 & 11   Hot Pads and
Bread Basket Liner

Project 12   Kaleidoscope Box

Resources

Look for these and other embroidery products at a local retailer where embroidery machines, software, and designs are sold. To find a dealer near you, contact these companies of interest.

Designs and Supplies

Ackfeld Wire
(888) 272-3135
www.ackfeldwire.com

Amazing Designs
(800) 443-8752
www.amazingdesigns.com

Cactus Punch
(800) 487-6972
www.cactuspunch.com

Charlescraft
www.charlescraft.com

EmbroideryArts
(888) 238-1372
www.embroideryarts.com

The Embroidery Resource
(800) 953-7656
www.embroideryresource.com

Judi & Co.
(631) 499-8480
www.judiandco.com

Kaleidoscope Kutz
kaleidokutz@msn.com

Nancy's Notions
(800) 833-0690
www.nancynotions.com

Oklahoma Embroidery Supply
& Design (OESD)
(800) 580-8885
www.embroideryonline.com

Sudberry House
(860) 739-6951
www.sudberry.com

Sulky Thread
Available through Speed
Stitch.
(800) 874-4115
www.speedstitch.com

Tina's Cross Stitch
(800) 237-0137, ext. 37
www.tinascrossstitch.com

OESD design

Embroidery Publications

Creative Machine Embroidery
(800) 677-5212
www.cmemag.com

Designs in Machine Embroidery
(888) SEW-0555
www.dzgns.com

Embroidery Journal
(480) 419-0167
www.embroideryjournal.com

Sew News
(800) 289-6397
www.sewnews.com

Embroidery Machine Companies

Baby Lock
(800) 422-2952
www.babylock.com

Bernina
(800) 405-2739
www.berninausa.com

Brother
(800) 422-7684
www.brother.com

Elna
(800) 848-3562
www.elnausa.com

Janome
(800) 631-0183
www.janome.com

Kenmore
(888) 809-7158
www.sears.com

Pfaff
(800) 997-3233
www.pfaff.com

Simplicity
(800) 553-5332
www.simplicitysewing.com

Singer
(800) 474-6437
www.singershop.com

Viking Sewing Machines
(800) 358-0001
www.husqvarnaviking.com

White
(800) 311-3164
www.whitesewing.com

Design Details

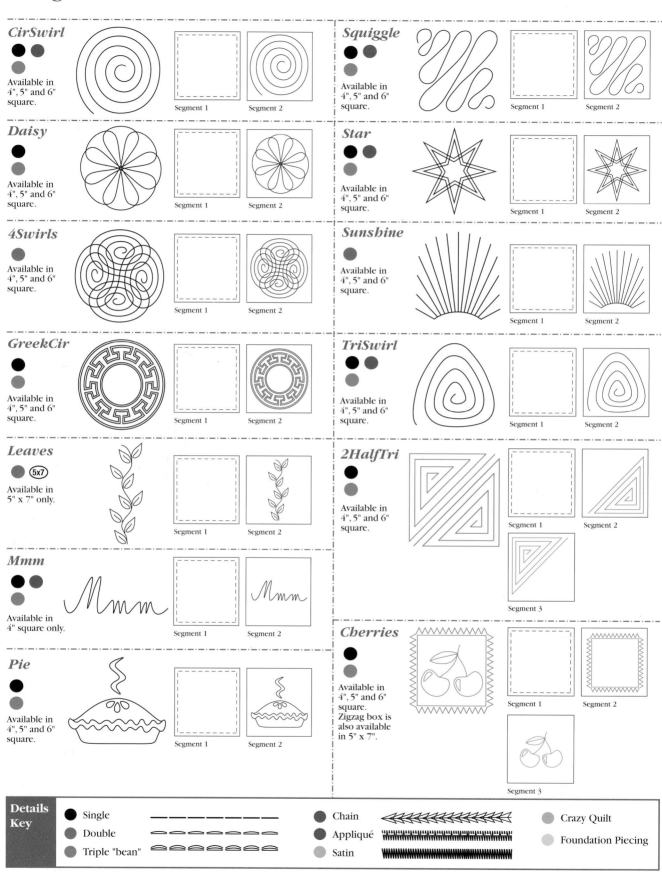

CirSwirl

Available in 4", 5" and 6" square.

Segment 1   Segment 2

Daisy

Available in 4", 5" and 6" square.

Segment 1   Segment 2

4Swirls

Available in 4", 5" and 6" square.

Segment 1   Segment 2

GreekCir

Available in 4", 5" and 6" square.

Segment 1   Segment 2

Leaves

5x7

Available in 5" x 7" only.

Segment 1   Segment 2

Mmm

Available in 4" square only.

Segment 1   Segment 2

Pie

Available in 4", 5" and 6" square.

Segment 1   Segment 2

Squiggle

Available in 4", 5" and 6" square.

Segment 1   Segment 2

Star

Available in 4", 5" and 6" square.

Segment 1   Segment 2

Sunshine

Available in 4", 5" and 6" square.

Segment 1   Segment 2

TriSwirl

Available in 4", 5" and 6" square.

Segment 1   Segment 2

2HalfTri

Available in 4", 5" and 6" square.

Segment 1   Segment 2

Segment 3

Cherries

Available in 4", 5" and 6" square. Zigzag box is also available in 5" x 7".

Segment 1   Segment 2

Segment 3

Details Key				
● Single	─ ─ ─ ─ ─	● Chain	◅◅◅◅◅◅◅◅◅	● Crazy Quilt
● Double	⌒⌒⌒⌒⌒⌒	● Appliqué	ʌʌʌʌʌʌʌʌ	○ Foundation Piecing
● Triple "bean"	⌒⌒⌒⌒⌒⌒	○ Satin	▮▮▮▮▮▮▮▮	

Design Details

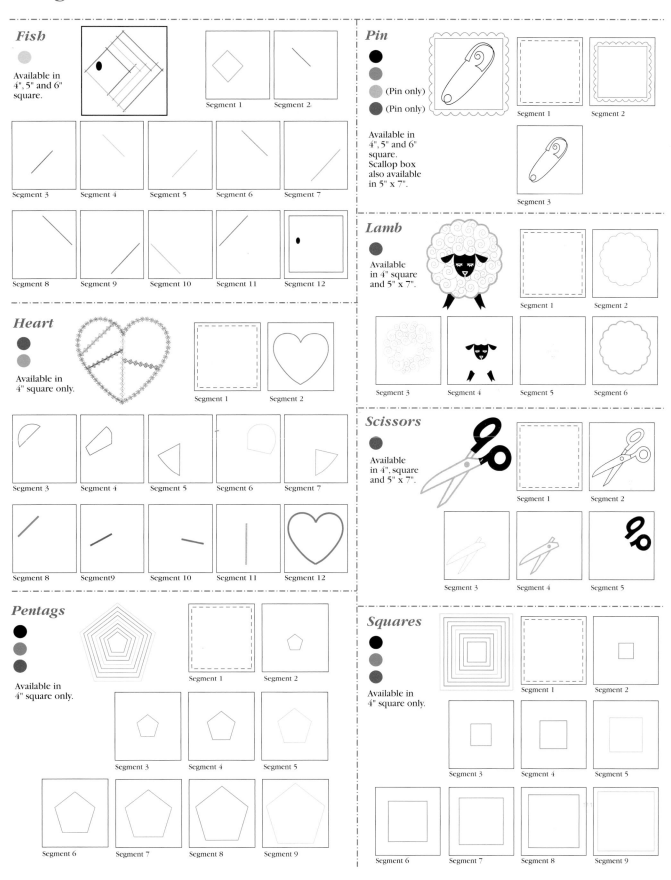

Fish

Available in 4", 5" and 6" square.

Segment 1 Segment 2

Segment 3 Segment 4 Segment 5 Segment 6 Segment 7

Segment 8 Segment 9 Segment 10 Segment 11 Segment 12

Heart

Available in 4" square only.

Segment 1 Segment 2

Segment 3 Segment 4 Segment 5 Segment 6 Segment 7

Segment 8 Segment 9 Segment 10 Segment 11 Segment 12

Pentags

Available in 4" square only.

Segment 1 Segment 2

Segment 3 Segment 4 Segment 5

Segment 6 Segment 7 Segment 8 Segment 9

Pin

(Pin only)
(Pin only)

Available in 4", 5" and 6" square. Scallop box also available in 5" x 7".

Segment 1 Segment 2

Segment 3

Lamb

Available in 4" square and 5" x 7".

Segment 1 Segment 2

Segment 3 Segment 4 Segment 5 Segment 6

Scissors

Available in 4", square and 5" x 7".

Segment 1 Segment 2

Segment 3 Segment 4 Segment 5

Squares

Available in 4" square only.

Segment 1 Segment 2

Segment 3 Segment 4 Segment 5

Segment 6 Segment 7 Segment 8 Segment 9

For more information on embroidery, purchase additional titles in this series: *Embroidery Machine Essentials, More Embroidery Machine Essentials, Companion Project Series: Basic Techniques,* and *Companion Project Series: Fleece Techniques.*

CD Instructions

The embroidery designs and graphic images featured in this book are located on the CD-ROM. You must have a computer and compatible embroidery software to access and utilize the decorative designs. Basic computer knowledge is helpful to understand how to copy the designs onto the hard-drive of your computer.

To access the designs, insert the CD-ROM into your computer. The designs are located on the CD-ROM in folders for each embroidery machine format. Copy the design files onto the computer hard-drive using one of the operating system (Windows) programs or open the design in applicable embroidery software. Be sure to copy only the design format compatible with your brand of embroidery equipment.

Once the designs are in your embroidery software or saved on your computer, transfer the designs to your embroidery machine following the manufacturer's instructions for your equipment. For more information about using these designs with your software or embroidery equipment, consult your owner's manual or seek advice from the dealer who honors your equipment warranty.